Rookie STAR™
Make a Difference

10 Things You Can Do To

Protect Animals

by Elizabeth Weitzman

Content Consultant
Lucy Spelman, D.V.M.

Reading Consultant
Jeanne M. Clidas, Ph.D.
Reading Specialist

Children's Press®
An Imprint of Scholastic Inc.

Table of Contents

Elephants, tigers, crocodiles, toucans...

We share the Earth with a lot of amazing animals. Unfortunately, humans are threatening their **habitats**. Many of these animals are becoming **endangered**. They might not be around much longer. The good news is that you can help! There are many ways you can protect animals.

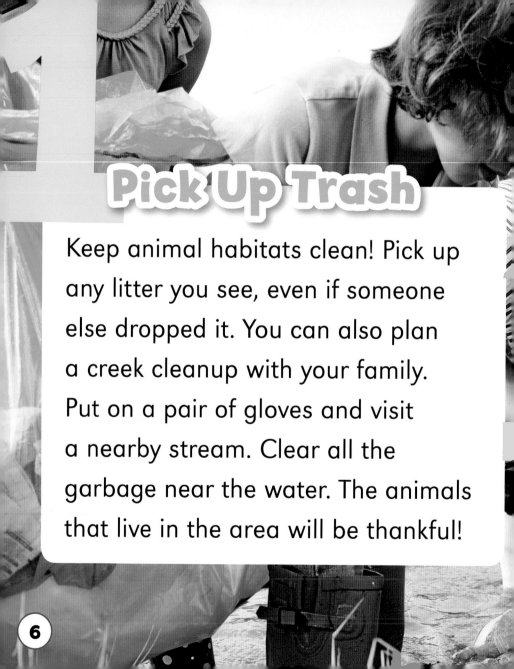

Pick Up Trash

Keep animal habitats clean! Pick up any litter you see, even if someone else dropped it. You can also plan a creek cleanup with your family. Put on a pair of gloves and visit a nearby stream. Clear all the garbage near the water. The animals that live in the area will be thankful!

Plastic bags can last for 1,000 years. And they are very dangerous for marine animals. More than 100,000 animals die each year from eating plastic or getting tangled up in bags. One easy way to help them is to stop using plastic bags at the grocery store.

Ask your parents to bring reusable bags whenever you go shopping.

Ask your principal if you can hang bird feeders around your school. You can even leave some pieces of yarn on a tree branch. It might be used to make a nest!

Honeybees pass pollen from one plant to another. This work, called **pollination**, is very important. It makes plants spread and grow. Some **pesticides** harm honeybees, and these hard-working animals are disappearing. Ask your parents to avoid using these dangerous chemicals in the garden.

Neighborhood

Bird feeders attract a variety of songbirds.

3 Make Your Yard

If you have a backyard, try to keep it as natural as possible. Make sure there are trees and bushes that can offer shelter all year long. Nuts and berries from

Chipmunks like to eat acorns.

Go Wild

these plants can feed animals. Chipmunks, owls, rabbits, and squirrels might make your backyard their home!

Woodpeckers store nuts in trees.

A lot of the world's animals live in forests. Many of these forests, especially rain forests, are being destroyed. Picture 150 football fields laid side by side. That is about 150 acres. It is the amount of rain forest that is lost every minute. Bengal tigers, jaguars, and spider monkeys (pictured) are some of the animals in danger of losing their homes.

Adopt a Shelter

Are you and your family planning to get a pet? It is better to adopt one from an animal shelter than to buy it

Dogs and cats are popular pets.

at a pet shop.
Shelter animals
have been abandoned.
They do not have another
safe place to go.

Pick the dog that is
right for your family.

Turtles can live for
100 years. That would
be a long time to care
for a pet!

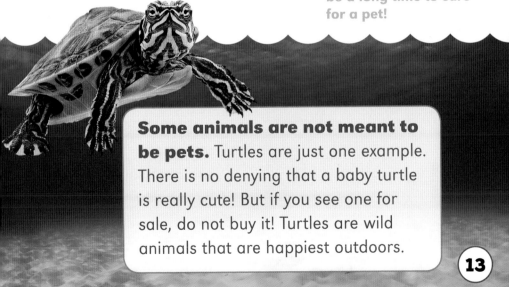

Some animals are not meant to be pets. Turtles are just one example. There is no denying that a baby turtle is really cute! But if you see one for sale, do not buy it! Turtles are wild animals that are happiest outdoors.

Pets need regular checkups from an animal doctor. Take your pet to the veterinarian. Ask him or her to tell you the best ways to feed and hold your animal. Make sure it always has plenty of fresh water.

Your vet can tell you how best to care for your pet.

Your vet may say your pets should be spayed or neutered. That means they will not be able to have babies. This is very important. There are too many unwanted pets in shelters already. An unspayed cat can have 100 kittens or more in her lifetime.

Home

Owning a pet is a
big responsibility!

Support an Animal Shelter

Can't adopt a pet? Adopt a shelter in your neighborhood instead!
Ask the people who work there what their animals need. You can collect food or toys for them. You can also visit the animals living there.
You might even be able to walk them or play with them.

Pets living in shelters need love and attention.

There are shelters for rabbits, horses, llamas, monkeys, and even elephants. These are often called sanctuaries. A sanctuary is a safe place, so it's a perfect name!

7 Buy Free-Range

Grocery stores carry a lot of different types of eggs. Some come from farms that keep the hens locked in tight cages. Others come from farms that give their hens more room to grow. Ask your parents to choose these "free-range" eggs.

Free-range chickens have had a better life than those that live in cages.

Eggs at the Store

Many farmers sell their food directly to people at outdoor farmers' markets. You can visit a market to buy eggs, cheese, milk, and other fresh foods. There is a good chance that the cows and chickens that provide these foods are not squished into tight cages.

Leave Endangered

Too many rare animals are taken out of their habitats. For example, coral belongs in the sea. But some people take it out of the ocean to make

Elephants live in large family groups called herds.

Animals Alone

jewelry or art.
Other people turn
seal fur into blankets
and coats. When we buy
these things, we put more
animals at risk.

A lot of people do
not realize that coral
is a living creature.

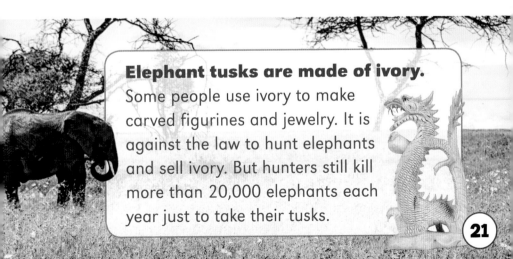

Elephant tusks are made of ivory.
Some people use ivory to make
carved figurines and jewelry. It is
against the law to hunt elephants
and sell ivory. But hunters still kill
more than 20,000 elephants each
year just to take their tusks.

Raise Money to

You can earn money from a lemonade stand or bake sale. Or set aside part of your allowance. You could even paint pictures of your favorite animals and have

A cool glass of lemonade tastes great on a hot day!

Help Animals

an art sale. Ask a parent or teacher to help you search for organizations that help animals. Then choose where you would like to send your donation.

If you like to draw, an art sale is a fun idea!

Isn't this koala cute? You can take care of one like it! Some wildlife organizations let kids "adopt" animals from all over the world. That means your money will help protect the animal in its natural habitat. You can even adopt a great white shark!

Visit farms, nature reserves, aquariums, and zoos. Learn about the creatures that live there. Then share what you have learned with friends and family. The more people know how to protect and love animals, the happier the animals on our planet will be!

Animal Life

A boy feeds sheep at a farm.

There are laws that help animals, too! In the U.S., the Endangered Species Act protects more than 1,000 animals, including bald eagles, grizzly bears, and gray wolves.

eaping to the Rescue

Are you wondering if kids really can make a difference?

The Prodigy Cats is an elementary school club in California that did. The members learned that California red-legged frogs were endangered. They thought the frogs would be safer if more people knew about them. So they decided to try to make the frog California's official state

State Amphibian: CA Red-legged Frog

amphibian. They visited the state capitol and talked to politicians about their plan. They asked friends and strangers to support it. After a lot of work, they got what they wanted. In 2015, the frog became the state's official amphibian! Now that the California red-legged frog is a state symbol, many more people will know about it and want to help protect it.

Wild animals that live in your area can find food and shelter in your yard. Here's an example of a garden habitat you might find in a backyard in New England.

Squirrels and birds build their nests in trees.

Monarch butterflies lay their eggs on milkweed plants.

Habitat

Small animals use bushes for protection from the weather and predators.

A bird feeder attracts a variety of songbirds.

Thyme

Parsley

Mint

Birds enjoy splashing around in a birdbath.

An herb garden attracts butterflies and bees.

29

Glossary

endangered (en-DAYN-jerd): in danger of becoming extinct

habitats (HAB-ih-tats): places where a plant or animal is usually found

pesticides (PESS-tih-sides): chemicals used to kill pests, such as insects

pollination (PAH-luh-nay-shun): the transfer of pollen from one flower to another to produce seeds

Index

About the Author

Elizabeth Weitzman is a longtime journalist and the author of more than 25 nonfiction books for children. She and her family live in Brooklyn, New York, with their beautiful blue betta fish, Jellybean. They are hoping to adopt a cat soon, too!

Facts for Now

Visit this Scholastic Web site for
more information on how to protect animals:

www.factsfornow.scholastic.com

Enter the keywords **Protect Animals**

Library of Congress Cataloging-in-Publication Data

Names: Weitzman, Elizabeth, author.
Title: 10 things you can do to protect animals / by Elizabeth Weitzman.
Other titles: Ten things you can do to protect animals
Description: New York, NY : Children's Press, an imprint of Scholastic Inc., [2017] | Series: Rookie star. Make a difference | Includes index.
Identifiers: LCCN 2016003663| ISBN 9780531226520 (library binding) | ISBN 9780531227589 (pbk.)
Subjects: LCSH: Wildlife conservation—Juvenile literature. | Habitat conservation—Juvenile literature.
Classification: LCC QH75 .W435 2017 | DDC 333.95/416—dc23
LC record available at http://lccn.loc.gov/2016003663

Produced by Spooky Cheetah Press
Design by Judith Christ-Lafond

© 2017 by Scholastic Inc.

Printed in China 62

2 3 4 5 6 7 8 9 10 R 25 24 23 22 21 20 19 18 17 16

Photographs ©: cover giraffe: Mattiaath/Dreamstime; cover elephant: Klein-Hubert/KimballStock; cover grass: Anan Kaewkhammul/Shutterstock, Inc.; cover yellow butterfly: kurga/iStockphoto/Thinkstock; cover red butterfly: Cezar Serbanescu/Getty Images; cover sky: Elenamiv/Shutterstock, Inc.; back cover grass: Anan Kaewkhammul/Shutterstock, Inc.; back cover yellow butterfly: kurga/iStockphoto/Thinkstock; back cover red butterfly: Cezar Serbanescu/Getty Images; 2 top left and throughout: Africa Studio/Shutterstock, Inc.; 2 top right and throughout: Ivan Vukovic/Shutterstock, Inc.; 2-3 grass and throughout: Fedorov Oleksiy/Shutterstock, Inc.; 3 elephant and throughout: Claudiad/iStockphoto; 4: skynesher/Getty Images; 5 top right: Martin Harvey/Getty Images; 5 center right: Yenyu Shih/Shutterstock, Inc.; 5 background: skynesher/Getty Images; 6: Leland Bobbé/Media Bakery; 7 background: Leland Bobbé/Media Bakery; 8: Konrad Wothe/Minden Pictures; 9: Buddy Mays/Alamy Images; 10 chipmunk: Eric Isselee/Shutterstock, Inc.; 10 acorns: Lorraine Swanson/Dreamstime; 11 top left: arka38/Shutterstock, Inc.; 11 top right: Steve & Dave Maslowski/Shutterstock, Inc.; 11 bottom right: Tony Camacho/Science Source; 12: skynesher/Getty Images; 13 bottom water: richcarey/iStockphoto; 13 bottom turtle: Gerald A. DeBoer/Shutterstock, Inc.; 13 top: Christopher Futcher/Getty Images; 14: Blaj Gabriel/Shutterstock, Inc.; 15: Ken Karp Photography; 16: M_a_y_a/Getty Images; 17 bottom right: David Hosking/Science Source; 17 background: M_a_y_a/Getty Images; 18 chickens: bonzami emmanuelle/Alamy Images; 19 background: Diana Taliun/Shutterstock, Inc.; 19 eggs: Diana Taliun/Shutterstock, Inc.; 20 bottom: Darren Bennett/Animals Animals; 21 top: Volodymyr Goinyk/Shutterstock, Inc.; 21 bottom right: Hemera Technologies/PhotoObjects.net/Thinkstck; 21 bottom background: Darren Bennett/Animals Animals; 22: Luke Miller/iStockphoto; 23 bottom left: ARZTSAMUI/Shutterstock, Inc.; 23 bottom right: Joanna Dorota/Shutterstock, Inc.; 23 top money: imagestock/iStockphoto; 23 top koala: Eric Isselee/Shutterstock, Inc.; 24: Monty Rakusen/Media Bakery; 25 top right: David Rasmus/Shutterstock, Inc.; 25 background: Monty Rakusen/Media Bakery; 26: Michael Durham/Minden Pictures; 27 center right: Ivan Valencuela; 27 background: Michael Durham/Minden Pictures; 28-29: Christina S. Wald, LLC; 30 center bottom: AndrisTkachenko/iStockphoto/Thinkstock; 30 top: Tony Camacho/Science Source; 30 bottom: Konrad Wothe/Minden Pictures; 30 center top: Darren Bennett/Animals Animals.